This book belongs to

_____

Dolly Parton

By Mary Nhin

This book is dedicated to my children - Mikey, Kobe, and Jojo.

Hi, I'm Dolly Parton.

I was born in 1946 in a small town in Tennessee.
I was the fourth child out of 12 children.

Life was hard because my family was poor and barely made ends meet.

My father worked various jobs to try to make enough money for our large family.

Even though times were difficult, I loved music.
I would sing at church and talent shows.

When I turned seven, I even made my own guitar to play while I sang!

I guess I made an impression on my Uncle Bob because he bought me my first guitar shortly after that. Uncle Bob was a songwriter. I was so excited to have my very first real guitar!

Thank you, Uncle!

You're welcome, Dolly!

Over time, I got popular and was invited to be on local talk shows and radio stations.

I released my first single at age 13 called "Puppy Love" for a small Louisiana label.

Even with that small success, I still had to work odd jobs to keep afloat. Times were tough as I didn't have any musical connections.

I still stayed hopeful about my dreams of becoming a music star. The day after high school graduation, I moved to Nashville, Tennessee.

The way I see it, if you want the rainbow, you gotta put up with the rain.

Soon after arriving in Nashville, I partnered with my uncle Bill. Life was still tough, but the rainbow was peaking out.

My initial success came as a songwriter. I wrote several hit singles for various artists.

One day, I was discovered by Porter Wagoner.

I joined Wagoner on his show. At first, the audience wasn't that happy that I was there, but slowly they began to like me.

I released "Jolene" and "I Will Always Love You" which both became hits.

I have sold more than 100 million records worldwide. 26 of my songs reached number one on the Billboard country charts, a record for a female artist.

The fame and success that I got in life never made me forget where I came from. I created a program called Imagination Library where I provide free books to children in need. It is still operating today.

I also give back to my community by supporting local schools and hospitals.

By reading about my life journey, my hope is that you will believe that your dreams and aspirations can come true with hard work and dedication. Never give up on your dreams!

Timeline

1956 – Dolly appears in talk shows and radio stations

1967 – Dolly makes album debut with *Hello, I'm Dolly*

1974 – Dolly releases song "I Will Always Love You"

1980 – Dolly appears in movie "9 to 5"

1995 – Dolly launches Imagination Library

1999 – Dolly is inducted into the Country Music Hall of Fame

minimovers.tv

 @marynhin   @officialninjalifehacks
#minimoversandshakers

 Ninja Life Hacks

 Mary Nhin   Ninja Life Hacks

 @officialninjalifehacks